AAT

Advanced Diploma Synoptic Assessment

Pocket Notes

These Pocket Notes support study for the following AAT qualifications:
AAT Advanced Diploma in Accounting – Level 3
AAT Advanced Certificate in Bookkeeping – Level 3
AAT Advanced Diploma in Accounting at SCQF Level 6

British library cataloguing-in-publication data

A catalogue record for this book is available from the British Library.

Published by:
Kaplan Publishing UK
Unit 2 The Business Centre
Molly Millars Lane
Wokingham
Berkshire
RG41 2QZ

ISBN 978-1-78740-306-2

© Kaplan Financial Limited, 2018

Printed and bound in Great Britain.

This Product includes content from the International Ethics Standards Board for Accountants (IESBA), published by the International Federation of Accountants (IFAC) in 2015 and is used with permission of IFAC.

Contents

Preface

These Pocket Notes contain the key points you need to know for the exam, presented in a unique visual way that makes revision easy and effective.

Written by experienced lecturers and authors, these Pocket Notes break down content into manageable chunks to maximise your concentration.

Quality and accuracy are of the utmost importance to us so if you spot an error in any of our products, please send an email to mykaplanreporting@kaplan.com with full details, or follow the link to the feedback form in MyKaplan.

Our Quality Co-ordinator will work with our technical team to verify the error and take action to ensure it is corrected in future editions.

A guide to the assessment

The assessment

All units within the Advanced Diploma in Accounting are mandatory. Four units are assessed individually in end of unit assessments, but this qualification also includes a synoptic assessment, sat towards the end of the qualification, which draws on and assesses knowledge and understanding from across the qualification.

Examination

ADSY is assessed by means of a computer based assessment. The CBA will last for 2 hours 45 minutes and will consist of two components.

In any one assessment, students may not be assessed on all content, or on the full depth or breadth of a piece of content. The content assessed may change over time to ensure validity of assessment, but all assessment criteria will be tested over time.

Learning outcomes & weighting

Assessment objective	Weighting
A01 Demonstrate an understanding of the relevance of the ethical code for accountants, the need to act ethically in a given situation and the appropriate action to take in reporting questionable behaviour	15%
A02 Prepare accounting records and respond to errors, omissions and other concerns, in accordance with accounting and ethical principles and relevant regulations	15%
A03 Apply ethical and accounting principles when preparing final accounts for different types of organisation, develop ethical courses of action and communicate relevant information effectively	15%
A04 Use relevant spreadsheet skills to analyse, interpret and report management accounting data	25%
A05 Prepare financial accounting information, comprising extended trial balances and final accounts for sole traders and partnerships, using spreadsheets	30%
Total	**100%**

Pass mark

To pass a unit assessment, students need to achieve a mark of 70% or more.

This unit contributes 35% of the total amount required for the Advanced Diploma in Accounting qualification.

Formatting

- Formatting.

Formatting

Formatting is a process whereby you change the visual aspects of your worksheet.

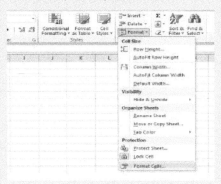

Number Changes number formats, for example the number of decimal places, currency type or percentages.

Alignment Allows adjustment of where data is shown within a cell for example left or right alignment, and merging cells together.

Font Appearance and size of text, along with special features like bold and underline.

Border Affects the cell itself, rather than the data within – place lines of varying size and colours around the cell.

Fill Colour the cell in various shades and patterns.

Protection Affects whether a cell can be edited.

To Exit the menu, click OK to accept any changes, or Cancel to reject them.

There are several shortcuts available on the **Home menu**.

Format number:

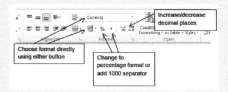

Alignment:

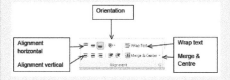

Font:

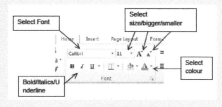

Borders:

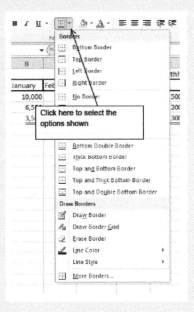

Other useful formatting options can be found on the **Page Layout** menu within **Page Setup**:

Margins:

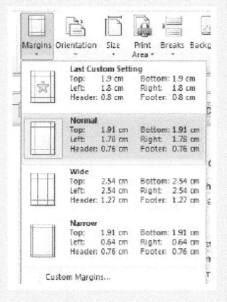

Print area:

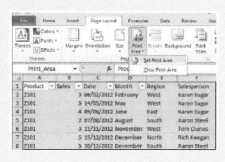

Fit to:

One of the most useful features regarding printing is the ability to specify how many pages you want your data to appear on.

Select **Fit to**

This can also be done via **Print** on the
File tab:

2

Formulae and functions

- Operators and order of preference.
- Using functions.
- The Insert Function button.
- Other functions.
- Logical functions.

Excel's primary purpose is to manipulate raw data through calculations and formulae. One of the main things you will use Excel for is simple calculations. The most basic calculations are the mathematical functions of addition +, subtraction -, multiplication * and divide /.

Operators and order of preference

Operator	Symbol	Order of Precedence
Brackets	()	1
Multiplication	*	2
Division	/	2
Addition	+	3
Subtraction	-	3

Using functions

To enter a function into a cell, always start with an **EQUALS SIGN** first.

You then type the **NAME** of the function, followed by an **OPEN BRACKET** (.

The **ARGUMENTS** of the function are then required. These tell Excel exactly what to do, and depend on the function required. If more than one argument is needed, they must be separated by a **COMMA**.

The function is ended with a **CLOSE BRACKET**).

The Insert Function button

The **Insert Function** button f_x located just above the column names:

Clicking this button brings up the **Insert Function** menu, which can help work out which function is required.

The most commonly used functions include:

=sum

=average

=max

=min

These can also be found by using the **Autosum** shortcut on the **Home** tab:

Other functions

ROUND

Instead of changing the format, you may wish to instruct Excel to round the numbers to a certain number of decimal places – this is often useful when dealing with currency – round to 2 decimal places. To do this, use the **ROUND** function:

=ROUND(number,num_digits)

- 'number' and 'num_digits' are the ARGUMENTS.
- **number** is the number or cell reference which needs rounding.
- **num_digits** is the number of decimal places you wish to round to.

The ROUND function follows normal mathematical rounding rules – 0-4 are rounded down and 5-9 are rounded up.

Sometimes you will want to force a number to be rounded up or down, and ROUNDUP or ROUNDDOWN will do this.

LOOKUPS

LOOKUPs can be used to interrogate large 'blocks' of data, and find the information required – linking the two together, so if the original is edited, the other spreadsheet will be too.

VLOOKUP

VLOOKUP is used when the data is in columns.

=VLOOKUP(lookup_value,table_array,col_ index_num,[range_lookup])

- **lookup_value** – this is the data item you are looking for.
- **table_array** – this is the range the data is in – i.e. where you are looking. The first column should contain the item being looked up and absolute

referencing needs to be added to ensure that Excel continues to look at the correct data if the vlookup is being used in more than one cell.

- **col_index_number** – this is the column number we want to use from the table_ array.
- **[range lookup]** – this should either be TRUE or FALSE. The square brackets indicate that this is an optional argument. If you leave it out then Excel will assume its value is TRUE.
- FALSE means that an exact match to the lookup_value must be found – useful for looking up specific items in a list.
- TRUE means the nearest value to the lookup_value will be found – useful if there is a range of values that the lookup_value lies between.

HLOOKUP

HLOOKUP is used when the data is in rows.

=HLOOKUP(lookup_value,table_array,row_index_num,[range_lookup])

- **Lookup_value** – this is the data item you are looking for.

- **Table_array** – this is the range the data is in – i.e. where you are looking. The first row should contain the item being looked up and absolute referencing needs to be added to ensure that Excel continues to look at the correct data if the hlookup is being used in more than one cell.

- **Row_index_num** – this is the row number we want to use from the table_array.

- **Range_lookup** – this should either be TRUE or FALSE. The square brackets indicate that this is an optional argument. If you leave it out then Excel will assume its value is TRUE.

- FALSE means that an exact match to the lookup_value must be found – useful for looking up specific items in a list.

- TRUE means the nearest value to the lookup_value will be found – useful if there is a range of values that the lookup_value lies between.

Logical functions

Logical Functions are very useful for What-If analysis within Excel. They can be used to check whether certain criteria have been met (like conditional formatting), and changing the calculation required as a result.

IF

IF is used to see a criteria has been met

=IF(logical_test,[value_if_true],[value_if_false])

- **Logical_test** – as above, a logical test is a test that will have the value TRUE or FALSE. What are we testing?

- **Value_if_true** – enter here what you would like to do if the test is true – this could be a calculation, some text or even another Excel function. What to do if the test is true.

- **Value_if_false** – enter here what to do if the test is false, in the same way. What to do if the test is false.

AND

AND is used when you want to check more than one thing is true. As it is a logical function, the result of an AND function will be TRUE or FALSE.

=AND([logical1,[logical2], ...)

OR

OR works in a similar way to AND, but this time we are checking is this true OR is this true OR is this true.

=OR(logical1,[logical2], ...)

3

Cell referencing

- Relative cell referencing.
- Absolute cell referencing.
- Mixed cell referencing.
- Referencing other worksheets.

There are three types of cell referencing:

Relative cell referencing

C4		f_x	=B2
	A	B	C	D
1				
2		10		
3				
4			10	
5				

The formula in cell C4 is = **B2**. This means that when the value in cell B2 is changed, C4 will be updated to show this (C4 is **LINKED** to B2).

With relative referencing like this, if you **Copy** and **Paste** the formula in cell C4 into another cell, the reference to B2 will change. The way it works is as follows:

- If you copy the formula **UP**, the row number decreases.

- If you copy the formula **DOWN**, the row number increases.

- If you copy the formula **RIGHT**, the column letter increases.

- If you copy the formula **LEFT**, the column letter decreases.

If we copy the formula into cell D3:

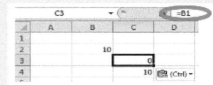

Here you can see the formula has been copied UP a row, so the row number in the reference has reduced by one. As there is no entry in cell B1, the result is shown as zero.

Absolute cell referencing

This is used to ensure that a formula always looks at the content of a particular cell or range of cells. This is very useful for V and H Lookups and 'what-if' analysis when you are looking at particular scenarios.

To create an **Absolute** reference we use a **$** sign before the letter and the number in the cell reference:

Mixed cell referencing

This is a combination of both **Absolute** and **Relative** referencing.

We want to calculate basic pay:

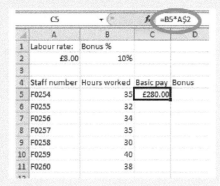

When the formula is copied down, the **$2** in the reference to cell A2 means that the row will remain fixed. You can copy the formula across, and the bonus is correctly calculated based on cell **B2** – because there is no $ before the A in the original formula, the column is not fixed.

	A	B	C	D
	D5		f_x	=C5*B$2
	A	B	C	D
1	Labour rate:	Bonus %		
2	£8.00	10%		
3				
4	Staff number	Hours worked	Basic pay	Bonus
5	F0254	35	£280.00	£28.00
6	F0255	32	£256.00	£25.60
7	F0256	34	£272.00	£27.20
8	F0257	35	£280.00	£28.00
9	F0258	30	£240.00	£24.00
10	F0259	40	£320.00	£32.00
11	F0260	38	£304.00	£30.40

Referencing other worksheets

It is very common that a calculation will need to refer to a cell on another worksheet within the same workbook. This works in the same way, but now instead of saying "Use the value in cell A1", we need to say "Use the value in Cell A1 on Sheet 2" (for example). The format for this would be:

='Sheet 2'!A1

The 'A1' part of the formula is referring to cell A1 – to specify the sheet name, use the quote marks, followed by an exclamation mark.

Remember that when entering a formula, you can click on the cell you wish to use rather than typing its reference. This is true whether the cell is on the current worksheet or not.

4

Conditional formatting

- Conditional formatting.

Conditional formatting

Conditional Formatting is where you can change the format of a cell based on certain conditions. For example you could want to colour a cell in red if its value is less than a certain number, or make the font bold if its value is equal to a number:

Clicking **New Rule** from the **Rules Manager** menu brings up the following options:

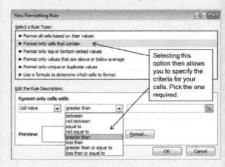

Set up the rule and the required formatting and click ok to apply.

It is possible to have up to 64 conditional formatting rules for any cell. Extra rules are added in the same way as a new rule – select the cells required and create a new rule.

Edit rules from within the **Rules Manager** box:

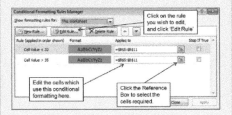

Use the **Rules Manager** to delete a rule in the same way. Alternatively, all rules can be deleted through the **Conditional Formatting** button in the **Home Menu**.

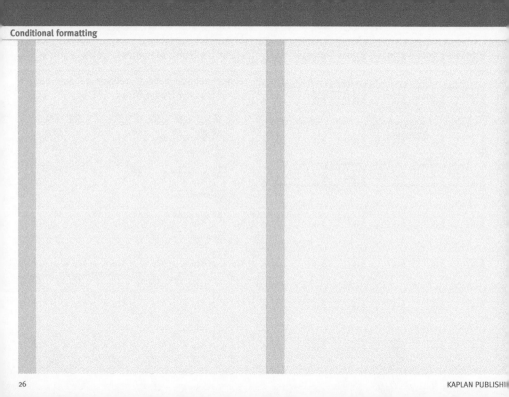

5

Charts and Graphs

- Basics.
- Creating a chart or graph.
- Formatting a chart or graph.

Basics

1. **Data Series** – these are the numbers [values] from which Excel is creating the graph. These are plotted on the **Value or 'Y' axis**.

2. **Category** – the information that identifies the data series. This is plotted along the **Category or 'X' axis**.

3. **Legend** – this identifies the different data series.

4. **Title** – gives meaning to the graph.

5. **Scale** – both the 'X' and the 'Y' axis (if numerical) can have a scale. These identify the range of values in the data series.

6. **Data Point** – this denotes the value of a particular data series. **Data Labels** can be placed next to data points to give greater meaning. Data Points have Data Markers. **Data Markers** are different shapes and colours for each data series.

Creating a chart or graph

Select the data you wish to graph, and on the Insert tab, select the chart type you want.

Formatting a chart or graph

Design tab

- Type – This allows you to change the type of chart you are using. The menu showing all available charts is shown, and can be selected in the same way as a new chart.

- Data – This is a very important menu. It allows you to change the data being used, or add new Series (data sets) to the chart.

- Layouts and Styles – This allows you to choose how the chart looks – the location of the title and legend and the colour scheme and general appearance of the chart.

- Move chart – This allows you to switch

between an embedded chart and a Chart Sheet. Simply click on the Move Chart button to change the location of your chart.

Layout Tab

This is where you can change many of the key visual features of your chart, such as titles and legends.

- Chart title – this allows you to add or remove a main Title for your chart. There are also options as to where and how the title is displayed.

- Axis titles – enables you to add or remove titles for both axes.

- Legend – the Legend is the 'key' which explains what the different colours or bars on the graph correspond to. Use this button to add or remove a Legend, as well as change the location of the Legend.

- Data labels – These show the actual

values of the data points on the graph. You can turn them on or off, as well as where they appear on the chart.

- Data table – A data table shows the actual data points being used to make the chart – like data labels but shown beneath the chart. Use this option to add/remove a data table, with or without a legend (key).

- Trend line – A trend line shows the general pattern of movement in your data set. Use the Trend Line button to do this. You will be presented with several options – normally you will choose Linear Trendline. The trendline will be added.

Format Tab

This tab allows you to change the format of any aspect of your graph – colours, thickness of lines and several other formatting options. Select (left-click on) the area of the graph you need to format and then select the option you need.

6

Pivot tables

- Pivot tables.

Pivot tables

A Pivot Table is a tool used for turning tables of data into meaningful reports. The tool can be used to create reports from external sources, multiple-workbooks (another consolidation tool) and workbooks.

To create a pivot table, select the data (including headers) you wish to use, then in the Insert tab, select Pivot Table.

This opens the **PivotTable Wizard**.

You can also choose whether to create the table in a new worksheet or place it somewhere on your existing sheet.

This view allows you to build your report. The following terms are used:

- **Fields** – are the data headings used to make the report.
- **Report Filter** – this is the 'pages' of the report. For example we might have a page for every month, or every product.

- **Row Labels** – the rows of our report.
- **Column Labels** – the columns in our report.
- **Σ Values** – this is the 'data' in our report – the results we would like to show.

There is an alternative way to create a Pivot Table, which many people feel is more user-friendly. This may be displayed by default, but if your screen looks like the previous screenshot, you could try Classic View, in the Options tab, select Options.

In the Display tab select Classic Layout for a more user-friendly method of creating the Table.

The appearance of the table changes – as it says, you can now 'drag and drop' the field names onto the table if you prefer. There is no difference in terms of the final appearance, but many people prefer this method.

Ethics – the principles

- The fundamental principles.
- Objectivity.
- Threats to independence.
- Safeguards.
- Professional competence and due care.
- Professional behaviour.
- Maintaining integrity.
- Confidentiality.
- The Institute of Business Ethics – Simple test.

The fundamental principles are likely to feature in your assessment.

You could be asked to apply a principle to a scenario.

The fundamental principles

Key Point

These principles are the fundamental underpinning to the syllabus and they must be learnt.

The fundamental principles are:

- **O**bjectivity – don't let your own bias or prejudice or pressure from others affect any decisions you make.

- **P**rofessional competence and due care – refuse to undertake any assignment that you are not competent to carry out and take the appropriate amount of care to ensure that the quality of the work performed meets the highest standards.

- **P**rofessional behaviour – don't act in any way that is unprofessional or does not comply with relevant laws and regulations.

- **I**ntegrity – being straightforward and honest in performing professional work and in all business relationships.

- **C**onfidentiality – only reveal confidential information with the client's authorisation or where there is a legal duty to disclose

Objectivity

Objectivity and Independence

Objectivity and threats to independence are likely to feature in your assessment.

The principle of objectivity goes hand-in-hand with the need for independence. The AAT guidelines stress that members must be both:

- Independent of mind.
- Independent in appearance.

Conflict of interest

Does a conflict of interest interfere with your objectivity/independence? Threats can be general or may relate to the specific circumstances of an engagement.

Threats to independence

The self-interest threat – may occur as a result of a financial or other interest held by the accountant or a family member.

The advocacy threat – may occur when an accountant promotes a position or opinion to the point where subsequent objectivity may be compromised.

The self-review threat – when a previous judgement needs to be re-evaluated – you cannot audit your own work.

The familiarity or trust threat – may occur when, because of a close relationship, the accountant becomes too sympathetic to the interests of others.

The intimidation threat – may occur when an accountant may be deterred from acting objectively by threats – actual or perceived.

Safeguards

Safeguards – are controls that mitigate or eliminate threats to independence.

Definition

Safeguards that may eliminate or reduce such threats to an acceptable level fall into two broad categories:

(i) Safeguards created by the profession, legislation or regulation.

(ii) Safeguards in the work environment.

Example

Examples of safeguards are;

- educational, training and experience requirements for entry into the profession

- Continuing Professional Development requirements

- corporate governance regulations

- professional standards

- professional or regulatory monitoring and disciplinary procedures

- external review of the reports, returns, communications or information produced by a member and carried out by a legally empowered third party.

Professional competence and due care

Professional accountants must refrain from performing any services that they are not competent to carry out unless appropriate advice and assistance is obtained to ensure that the services are performed satisfactorily.

Members have a responsibility to:

- Follow relevant laws and regulations.
- Maintain their professional competence.
- Prepare complete and clear reports and recommendations.

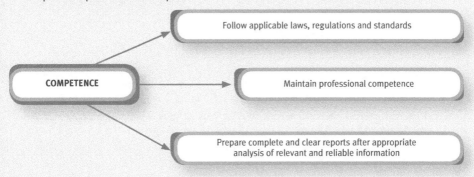

COMPETENCE

Follow applicable laws, regulations and standards

Maintain professional competence

Prepare complete and clear reports after appropriate analysis of relevant and reliable information

Professional behaviour

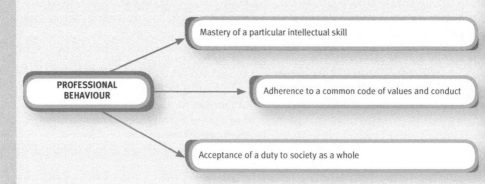

- Credibility – there is a need for credibility in information and information systems.
- Professionalism – there is a need to be clearly identified as a professional person in the following areas
  - Client relations.
  - Professional courtesy.
  - Expertise.

Maintaining integrity

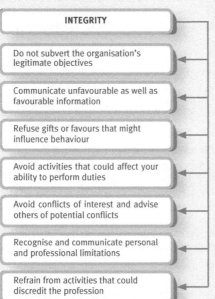

INTEGRITY

Do not subvert the organisation's legitimate objectives

Communicate unfavourable as well as favourable information

Refuse gifts or favours that might influence behaviour

Avoid activities that could affect your ability to perform duties

Avoid conflicts of interest and advise others of potential conflicts

Recognise and communicate personal and professional limitations

Refrain from activities that could discredit the profession

Confidentiality

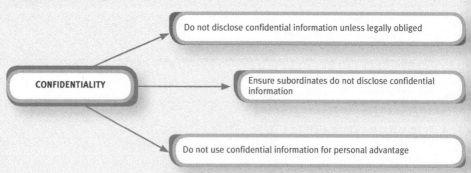

CONFIDENTIALITY

Do not disclose confidential information unless legally obliged

Ensure subordinates do not disclose confidential information

Do not use confidential information for personal advantage

Disclosure of confidential information

In certain cases the law specifically requires disclosure of confidential information. One particular area is money laundering, which includes possessing or in any way dealing with or concealing the proceeds of any crime.

Assessment focus

A possible assessment scenario could ask you whether you think the information held by you should be disclosed or kept from disclosure.

The key thought process here would be to ask the question "What is in the public interest?"

When does confidentiality apply?

Members should refrain from:

- disclosing confidential information without proper and specific authority or unless there is a legal or professional right or duty to disclose and

- using confidential information to their personal advantage or the advantage of third parties.

Disclosure may be appropriate:

(a) where **permitted** by law and authorised by the client.

(b) where **required** by law (e.g. disclosure of money laundering).

(c) where there is a professional **duty** to disclose, which is in the public interest, and is not prohibited by law. (e.g. to protect the member's professional interests in legal proceedings).

The Institute of Business Ethics – Simple test

An individual's ethical decision could be stated in answering the following questions:

Element	Explanation
Transparency	Do I mind others knowing what I have decided?
Effect	Does my decision affect or hurt anyone?
Fairness	Would my decision be considered fair by those affected?

8

Professional considerations

- The objectives of the accounting profession.
- Rules and principle based approaches to codes of ethics.
- Keeping up to date.
- The CPD development cycle.
- Disciplinary process.

The objectives of the accounting profession

The objectives of the accounting profession features in the sample paper and is therefore likely to be examined frequently.

The accountancy profession is committed to the following objectives:

- the mastering of particular skills and techniques acquired through learning and education and maintained through continuing professional development

- development of an ethical approach to work as well as to employers and clients. This is acquired by experience and professional supervision under training and is safeguarded by strict ethical and disciplinary guidelines

- acknowledgement of duties to society as a whole in addition to duties to the employer or the client

- an outlook which is essentially objective, obtained by being fair minded and free from conflicts of interest

- rendering services to the highest standards of conduct and performance

- achieving acceptance by the public that members provide accountancy services in accordance with these high standards and requirements.

Responsibility to the public – public interest

A professional accountant's responsibility is not exclusively to satisfy the needs of an individual client or employer. A distinguishing mark of a profession is acceptance of its responsibility to the public who rely on its objectivity and integrity to maintain the orderly functioning of commerce.

- Financial managers contribute to the efficient and effective use of the organisation's resources.

- Internal auditors provide assurance about a sound internal control system which enhances the reliability of the external financial information.

- Independent auditors help to maintain the integrity and efficiency of the financial statements.

- Tax experts help to establish confidence and efficiency in, and the fair application of the tax system.

- Management consultants have a responsibility toward the public interest in advocating sound management decision-making.

Rules and principle based approaches to codes of ethics

The IFAC and AAT codes adopt a principles-based approach.

They do not attempt;

- To cover every situation where a member may encounter professional ethical issues.
- Prescribe the way in which he or she should respond.

Instead, they adopt a value system, focusing on fundamental professional and ethical principles which are at the heart of proper professional behaviour and which members must therefore follow.

The conceptual framework

This conceptual framework approach requires members to identify, evaluate and respond to threats to compliance with the fundamental principles.

Principle-based (integrity) approach

You look at the objective to be achieved and focus on it. The AAT states the fundamental principles that must be observed. They are the profession's firm guideposts.

Rule-based (compliance) approach

You apply the rules exactly as stated, regardless of the circumstances. The law defines the minimum ethical standards in a given area of practice and government regulations outline what is acceptable and what is not.

Keeping up to date

Ethical principle of Professional Competence requires accountants to have up-to-date technical knowledge.

Accountants need to keep up to date with changes in the following areas:

- reporting and auditing standards;
- ethical codes;
- tax and companies legislation;
- relevant criminal law including bribery, fraud, money laundering;
- regulation of accounting, reporting, tax compliance, audit, the accountancy and finance profession.

Continuing professional development

Types of CPD

There are two strands to CPD:

- Update CPD, which ensures professional competence and prevents technical obsolescence within the member's field of work.
- Developmental CPD, which provides new knowledge, broadens skills and opens up new career opportunities.

Structured and unstructured CPD

Structured CPD	Unstructured CPD
• In-house training	• Reading professional / technical articles
• Other professional bodies	• Educational videos
• University courses	• Specific reading material that relates to practical work
• Conferences both local and international	• Distance learning (with no assessment)
• Branch courses	
• National courses	
• Assessed distance learning	
• Outside providers	
• Other structured courses	

Why do CPD?

- maintain high professional standards for you and your team

- be more flexible and adapt to change/new opportunities

- adapt and move into new areas of practice

- develop the skills to set up or expand your own practice

- get into a better position for promotion

- help your existing organisation to become more successful

- give the best possible service (to colleagues and customers)

- get more enjoyment and personal satisfaction from your work

- help and support others more, e.g. colleagues, family and community.

The CPD development cycle

The 4 steps of the CPD development cycle is a must learn.

The development cycle is a 4 step process:

- Assess.
- Plan.
- Action.
- Evaluate.

AAT members are expected to complete the CPD cycle twice a year.

Disciplinary process

The AAT's disciplinary process is focused on;

'Maintaining public confidence in the accountancy profession upholding the standards of Conduct & Compliance that we expect from our members'.

In the case of proven malpractice by a full or fellow member (but not an affiliate or student member) that he or she:

- be expelled from the Association
- have his/her membership of the Association suspended
- have his/her practising Licence withdrawn
- be declared ineligible for a practising licence
- have his/her fellow member status removed (if applicable)
- be severely reprimanded

- be fined a sum not exceeding such maximum figure as the Council may set from time to time

- give a written undertaking to refrain from continuing or repeating the misconduct in question.

In the case of an affiliate or student member (but not a full or fellow member) that he or she:

- be declared unfit to become a full member

- have his/her registration as a student withdrawn

- be severely reprimanded

- be fined a sum not exceeding such maximum figure as the Council may set from time to time

- be debarred from sitting the Association's assessments for such period as shall be determined

- have a relevant assessment result declared null and void

- give a written undertaking to refrain from continuing or repeating the misconduct in question.

9

Legal considerations – I

- What is money laundering?
- Knowledge or suspicion.
- Offences.
- Customer due diligence.
- Whistle blowing.

What is money laundering?

Money laundering is another very popular area to include in a scenario.

- In UK law money laundering includes all forms of handling or possessing **criminal property**, including possessing the proceeds of one's own crime, and facilitating any handling or possession of **criminal property**.

- Materiality or **de minimis** exceptions are not available in relation to either **money laundering** or **terrorist financing** offences, meaning no amount is too small not to bother about.

Regulation

UK anti-money laundering regime requirements are set out in the:

- Proceeds of Crime Act 2002 (POCA).
- Money Laundering Regulations 2007.
- Terrorism Act 2000 & 2006.

Under the POCA, there are three money laundering offences:

- s327 – Concealing, disguising, converting, transferring or removing criminal property.
- s328 – Taking part in an arrangement to facilitate the acquisition, use or control of criminal property.
- s329 – Acquiring, using or possessing criminal property.

Money laundering offences

Anyone can commit a money laundering offence.

Conviction of any of these offences is punishable by up to 14 years imprisonment and/or an unlimited fine.

A person commits a money laundering offence if he:

- **Conceals**, disguises, converts or transfers criminal property, or removes criminal property from England and Wales, or from Scotland or from Northern Ireland.

- Enters into or becomes concerned in an **arrangement** which he knows **or suspects** facilitates (by whatever means) the acquisition, retention, use or control of criminal property.

- **Acquires**, uses or has possession of criminal property except where adequate consideration was given for the property.

Knowledge or suspicion

Knowledge or suspicion?

An offence is committed by an individual in the **regulated sector** if he fails to report where he has knowledge, suspicion or reasonable grounds for suspecting money laundering activity.

There is no definition of knowledge or suspicion and so interpretation of their meaning will rely on judgements in past legal cases.

- Having knowledge means actually knowing that something is the case.

- Case law suggests that suspicion is a state of mind more definite than speculation, but falls short of knowledge based on evidence.

Procedure for reporting known or suspected money laundering.

Assessment focus

The mnemonics MLRO And NCA must be understood in full.

A Suspicious Activity Report or (SAR) is made promptly to:

- An Internal Money Laundering Reporting Officer (MLRO).

However if no such role exists within the organisation then:

- Direct to the National Crime Agency (NCA).

Required Disclosure

- The identity of the suspect (if known).

- The information or other matter on which the knowledge or suspicion of money laundering (or reasonable grounds for such) is based.

- The whereabouts of the laundered property (if known).

- Additional information held by the individual which identifies other parties involved in, or connected to, the matter.

There is a standard form for reporting to NCA.

Offences

Failure to disclose

Individuals in the **regulated sector** commit an offence if they fail to make a disclosure in cases where they have knowledge or suspicion, or reasonable grounds for suspicion, that **money laundering** are occurring.

Disclosure must be made to their **MLRO** or direct to **NCA**.

This offence is punishable by imprisonment of up to 14 years and/or an unlimited fine.

Tipping off

The offence of **Tipping off** is making any disclosure which he knows or suspects are likely to prejudice any investigation that might follow that report.

The penalty for this offence is a maximum of 5 years imprisonment, or an unlimited fine, or both.

A tipping off disclosure may be made in writing or verbally, and either directly or indirectly.

Criminal property may take any form, including in money or money's worth, securities, tangible property and intangible property.

Also taken to encompass activities relating to **terrorist financing**, including handling or possessing funds to be used for terrorist purposes as well proceeds from terrorism.

Customer due diligence

Assessment focus

Before entering a client relationship an adequate customer due diligence must be carried out by:

- Identifying the client and verifying the client's identity on the basis of documents, data or information obtained from a reliable source.

Members in practice must assess the risk of their services being used to facilitate money laundering or terrorist financing.

Whistle blowing

Whistle blowing means disclosing information that a worker believes is evidence of:

- illegality
- gross waste
- gross mismanagement
- abuse of power
- substantial and specific danger to the public health and safety.

Internal and external whistle blowing

Some organisations have internal phone lines or email addresses for employees to report concerns without fear of reprisals

The Public Interest Disclosure Act, 1998 gives protection including protection from dismissal, to employees in the UK who disclose otherwise confidential information to a prescribed regulator in good faith.

10

Legal considerations – II

- Operational risk.
- Bribery.
- Fraud.

Operational risk

What is operational risk?

Definition

It has been defined broadly as:

'The risk of losses resulting from inadequate or failed internal processes, people and systems, or external events'

Operational risks include risks of fraud, theft and employee malfeasance.

Bribery

Bribery Act 2010

Offences under the Bribery Act

- Active bribery: promising or giving financial or other advantage.
- Passive bribery: agreeing to receive or accepting financial or other advantage.
- Bribery of foreign public officials.

- The failure of commercial organisations to prevent bribery by an associated person (corporate offence).

Companies can be liable for bribery committed for their benefit by their employees or other associated persons, even if they had no knowledge of those actions.

There is also personal liability for senior company officers that turn a blind eye to bribery.

Penalty

Imprisonment for up to ten years with an unlimited fine.

Defence

The company can use the defence that it 'had in place adequate procedures designed to prevent persons associated with the company from undertaking such conduct'.

Fraud

Fraud is a common topic in scenario questions.

What is fraud?

Definition

'Dishonestly obtaining an advantage, avoiding an obligation or causing a loss to another party'.

A distinction needs to be made between:

- Fraud, which is deliberate falsification, and
- Errors, which are unintentional mistakes.

The size of fraud risk for any organisation is a factor of:

- The probability of fraud occurring, and
- The size of the losses if fraud does occur.

A bank will be subject to much higher fraud risk than a property investment company due to the desirability of money and the potential value that theft could achieve; It is unlikely that someone will steal a building from an investment company.

Example

Examples of fraud

- The theft of cash or other assets.

- False accounting: this includes concealing or falsifying accounting records with a view to personal gain or providing false information that is misleading or deceptive.

- Crimes against consumers or clients, e.g. misrepresenting the quality of goods, pyramid trading schemes, selling counterfeit goods.

- Employee fraud against employers, e.g. payroll fraud, falsifying expense claims, theft of cash.
- Crimes against investors, consumers and employees, e.g. financial statement fraud.
- Crimes against financial institutions, e.g. using lost and stolen credit cards, fraudulent insurance claims.
- Crimes against government, e.g. social security benefit claims fraud, tax evasion.
- Crimes by professional criminals, e.g. money laundering.
- E-crime by people using computers, e.g. spamming, copyright crimes, hacking.

Fraud risk should be managed by:

The management of fraud risk should be a fundamental element of organisation's internal control system.

Consisting of two key areas:

- Fraud prevention: ensuring that the opportunities to commit fraud are minimised.
- Fraud detection and deterrence: detection measures are designed to identify fraud after it has occurred. If employees fear that the risk of detection is high, they will be deterred from trying to commit fraud.

Employee malfeasance risk

Malfeasance means doing wrong or committing an offence. Organisations might be exposed to risks of actions by employees that result in an offence or crime (other than fraud). This, like fraud risk, is a type of operational business risk.

Examples of employee malfeasance are:

- Illegal activities by employees should be controlled by suitable internal controls, to ensure that employees comply with established policies and procedures.
- Failing to comply with statutory requirements.

The Fraud Act (2006)

Fraud is a criminal act and can be broken down into three distinct offences.

Fraud by false representation

"Any representation as to fact or law ... express or implied" which they know to be untrue or misleading.

Fraud by failing to disclose information

Failure to disclose any information to a third party when they are under a legal duty to disclose such information.

Fraud by abuse of position

Where a person occupies a position where they are expected to safeguard the financial interests of another person, and abuses that position.

In all three classes of fraud, for an offence to have occurred, the person must have acted dishonestly, and with the intent of making a gain for themselves or anyone else, or inflicting a loss (or a risk of loss) on another.

The accountant in practice

- Overview.
- Accepting work.
- Tax services.

Overview

Your assessment will examine you on your ability to identify unethical behaviour and act accordingly.

There are many situations which the examiners could draw on, however previous assessments have included questions on fees charged, holding monies and misleading advertisements.

Accepting work

Technical competence

A professional accountant in practice should work within the confines of their own professional experience, knowledge and expertise, and of the client engagement.

If in doubt regarding competence then seek advice about such concerns from an employer's confidential helpline or an appropriate professional body.

Independence/objectivity

To ensure objectivity is not compromised, you should avoid:

- Owning shares in client companies.

- Allowing relatives and close friends to own shares in client companies.

- Giving or receiving a loan to a client (includes allowing client to have huge fees outstanding).

- Having a joint venture with a client.

- Being a trustee of any estate that has a financial interest in the client.

Personal and family relationships can also affect your independence (self interest threat).

You must not audit accounts that you have prepared (self review threat to objectivity).

You should be careful when receiving gifts, discounts or excessive hospitality as these may create self-interest and familiarity threats.

Managing potential liability

- Identify the terms of the engagement
- Define the specific tasks to be undertaken
- Define the responsibilities to be undertaken by the client
- Specify any limitations on the work to be undertaken
- Take out professional indemnity insurance
- Carry out customer due diligence
- Check with existing/previous accountant if there are any professional reasons why the appointment should not be accepted.

Tax services

Acceptance of tax clients

The key ethical issues relating to undertaking tax work are as follows:

- A member should not hold out to a client or an employer the assurance that any tax return prepared and tax advice offered are beyond challenge.

- A member should only undertake taxation work on the basis of full disclosure by the client or employer.

Dealing with errors and omissions

In tax engagements it is likely that errors and omissions will be discovered. The ethical issue is how you deal with those errors and omissions. For example, a client might put an accountant under pressure not to disclose adjustments that would increase their tax liability. The relevant guidance is as follows:

A member should not be associated with any return or communication in which there is reason to believe that it:

- contains a false or misleading statement

- contains statements or information furnished recklessly or without any real knowledge of whether they are true or false or

- omits or obscures information required to be submitted and such omission or obscurity would mislead the tax authorities.

In the case of a member in practice, acting for a client, the member should furnish copies of all tax computations to the client before submitting them to HMRC.

Material error disclosure

When a member learns of a material error or omission in a tax return of a prior year, or of a failure to file a required tax return, the member has a responsibility to advise promptly the client or employer of the error or omission and recommend that disclosure be made to HMRC.

If the client or employer, after having had a reasonable time to reflect, does not correct the error, the member should inform the client or employer in writing that it is not possible for the member to act for them in connection with that return or other related information submitted to the authorities.

Funds dishonestly retained after discovery of an error or omission become criminal property and their retention amounts to money laundering by the client or employer.

It is also a criminal offence in the UK for a person, including an accountant, to become concerned in an arrangement which he knows or suspects facilitates (by whatever means) the acquisition, retention, use or control of criminal property by or on behalf of another person.

A member in practice whose client refuses to make disclosure of an error or omission to HMRC, after having had notice of it and a reasonable time to reflect, is obliged to report the client's refusal and the facts surrounding it to the MLRO if the member is within a firm, or to the appropriate authority (NCA in the UK).

12

Sustainability

- Definitions.
- Triple Bottom Line (TBL) reporting.
- The role and responsibilities of finance professionals.

Definitions

- Sustainable development is development that meets the needs of the present without compromising the ability of future generations to meet their own needs (The UN's Bruntland Report).

- A sustainable business is a business that offers products and services that fulfil society's needs while placing an equal emphasis on people, planet and profits. (The Sustainable Business Network).

Note: sustainability is more than just looking at environmental concerns. It relates to the continuity of economic, social and environmental aspects of human society.

It is ethically wrong for this generation to benefit at the expense of future generations.

Triple Bottom Line (TBL) reporting

- TBL accounting expands the traditional company reporting framework to take into account environmental and social performance in addition to financial (economic) performance.

- Looks at reporting performance and decision making.

- The concept is also explained using the triple 'P' headings of 'People, Planet and Profit'.

The role and responsibilities of finance professionals

Professional accountants have a responsibility to act in the public interest. This includes supporting sustainability and sustainable development and considering the risks to society as a whole of not acting sustainably.

Finance professionals will typically be involved in the following:

- Creating an ethics-based culture
- Championing and promoting sustainability
- Risk management
- Performance management.

13

Recap of key aspects of Management Accounting – Costing

- Financial accounting and management accounting.
- The nature of cost accounting.
- Cost classification.
- Pricing issues of raw materials.
- Cost of holding inventory.
- Holding costs.
- Systems of inventory control.
- Inventory control levels.
- Labour costs – Remuneration systems.
- Direct and indirect labour costs.
- Direct and indirect expenses.
- Basic variance analysis.
- Overhead allocation and apportionment.
- Methods of reapportionment.
- Absorption of overheads.

- Under/over absorption of overheads.
- Absorption costing.
- Marginal costing.
- Marginal vs absorption costing.
- Activity Based Costing.
- Job, batch and service costing.
- Basics of process costing.
- Normal losses and abnormal loss and gains.
- Scrap value.
- Equivalent units and work in progress.
- Relevant costing.
- CVP Analysis.
- Breakeven analysis.
- Limiting factors.
- Net present value.
- Internal rate of return.

Financial accounting and management accounting

Financial accounts are an historical record of transactions which are presented in a standard format laid down by law. Such accounts are normally produced once or twice a year and are primarily used by external groups, e.g. shareholders.

Management accounts can be produced in any format that is useful to an organisation. They tend to be produced more frequently than financial accounts, usually once a month. They contain information required to run a business.

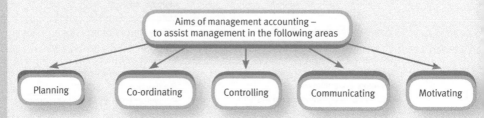

Aims of management accounting – to assist management in the following areas

| Planning | Co-ordinating | Controlling | Communicating | Motivating |

The nature of cost accounting

Definition

Cost accounting is the process of calculating and recording the costs involved in the production and distribution of products and services.

Main reason for carrying out cost accounting: to calculate the cost of a product and therefore set the sales price of the item.

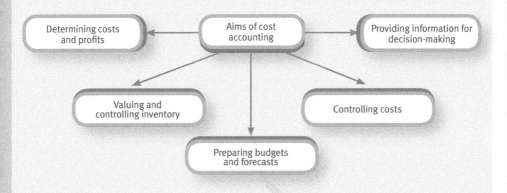

Cost classification

Cost can be classified as follows:

Classification	Purpose
By element – materials, labour and expenses	Cost control
By function – production (cost of sales), and non-production (distribution costs, administrative expenses)	Financial accounts
By nature – direct and indirect	Cost accounts
By behaviour – fixed, variable, stepped fixed and semi-variable	Budgeting, decision making

Pricing issues of raw materials

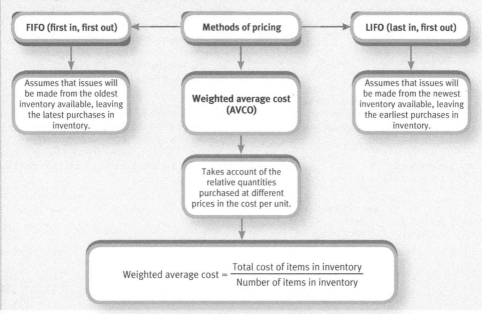

FIFO (first in, first out) ← Methods of pricing → LIFO (last in, first out)

FIFO: Assumes that issues will be made from the oldest inventory available, leaving the latest purchases in inventory.

Weighted average cost (AVCO)

LIFO: Assumes that issues will be made from the newest inventory available, leaving the earliest purchases in inventory.

Takes account of the relative quantities purchased at different prices in the cost per unit.

$$\text{Weighted average cost} = \frac{\text{Total cost of items in inventory}}{\text{Number of items in inventory}}$$

Cost of holding inventory

Functions of inventory

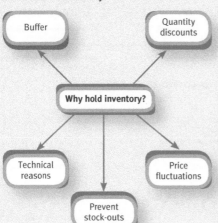

Inventory control

Inventory **control**: the method of ensuring that the right quantity of the right quality of the relevant inventory is available at the right time and in the right place.

CBA focus

There are a number of formulae associated with calculating inventory control levels – they are not provided in your assessment and so it is important that you learn them by heart.

Holding costs

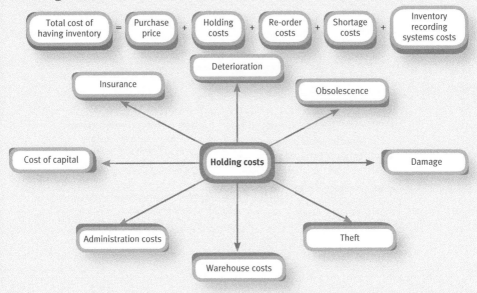

Total cost of having inventory = Purchase price + Holding costs + Re-order costs + Shortage costs + Inventory recording systems costs

Insurance

Deterioration

Obsolescence

Cost of capital

Holding costs

Damage

Administration costs

Warehouse costs

Theft

Systems of inventory control

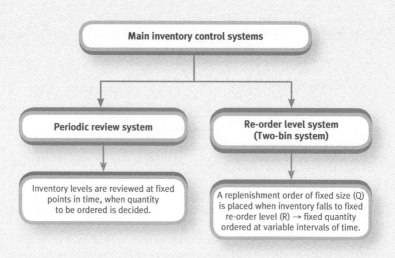

Main inventory control systems

Periodic review system

Re-order level system (Two-bin system)

Inventory levels are reviewed at fixed points in time, when quantity to be ordered is decided.

A replenishment order of fixed size (Q) is placed when inventory falls to fixed re-order level (R) → fixed quantity ordered at variable intervals of time.

Inventory control levels

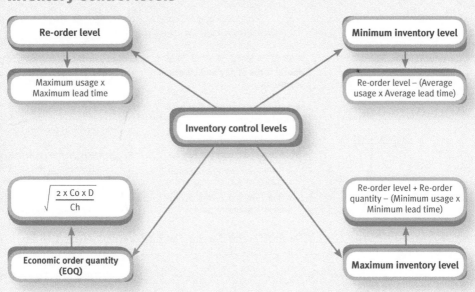

Re-order level

Maximum usage x Maximum lead time

Minimum inventory level

Re-order level – (Average usage x Average lead time)

Inventory control levels

$$\sqrt{\frac{2 \times Co \times D}{Ch}}$$

Economic order quantity (EOQ)

Re-order level + Re-order quantity – (Minimum usage x Minimum lead time)

Maximum inventory level

Labour costs – Remuneration systems

```
REMUNERATION SYSTEMS
```

Annual salaries
tend to be paid to managers and non-production staff

Gross pay (per month)

$$= \frac{\text{Annual salary}}{12}$$

Hourly rates of pay and overtime payments

Mainly apply to production and manual workers.

- Paid for every hour worked.
- Standard hours per week.
- Hours worked in excess of standard = Overtime hours.
- Overtime pay = Basic pay + Overtime premium.

Piecework payments
are made when a fixed constant amount is paid per unit of output.

Disadvantages of this system include no security of income and being penalised for low levels of output which occur for reasons beyond an employee's control (e.g. machine breakdown). To overcome these disadvantages, the straight piecework rate is often accompanied by a **guaranteed minimum payment**.

Direct and indirect labour costs

Direct labour costs	Indirect labour costs
↓	↓
Production workers' wages	Managers' and supervisors' salaries
↓	Overtime premium when overtime worked due to general pressure of work.
Overtime premium when overtime worked at the specific instruction of a customer	Holiday pay
	Training time
	Controllable idle time

Definition

Idle time: non-productive hours that are paid for.

Key Point

The distinction between direct and indirect labour costs is a very important one.

Direct and indirect expenses

Definition

All of the costs incurred by an organisation which are not materials or labour are known as **expenses**.

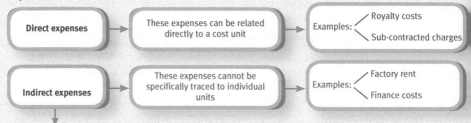

Also known as **overheads**

- **Production overheads** may be accounted for as part of cost of sales (factory rent, insurance, light and heat costs).
- **Non-production overheads** may be accounted for below the gross profit line (administrative costs, selling and distribution costs).
- NOTE: In the real world the term "expenses" could include both direct and indirect components. In the exam, however, expenses are always treated simply as 'overheads' with no separation into direct and indirect elements.

Basic variance analysis

The aim is to be able to compare the costs and revenues of the activity that has actually been completed with what revenue and cost that level of activity should have produced. To be able to make this comparison a flexed budget needs to be produced.

Flexed budgets

A flexed budget calculates the costs and revenues at certain levels of activity based on the budget costs.

To be able to produce a flexed budget a good knowledge of cost behaviours is required – see chapter 2.

Overview of cost behaviours:

- Variable – increases in direct proportion with the level of activity and is constant per unit.
- Fixed – remains constant in total at all levels of activity.
- Stepped – remains constant in total to a certain level of activity and then the cost steps up to a new higher constant.
- Semi-variable – there is a fixed element to the cost and a variable element. These costs are separable using the high-low method.

Overhead allocation and apportionment
Reapportionment

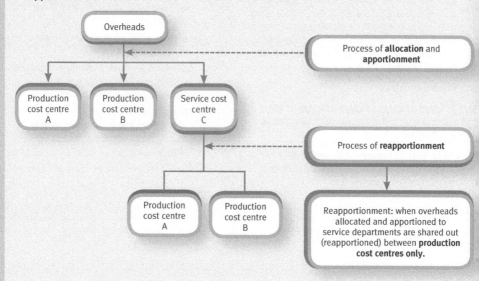

Methods of reapportionment

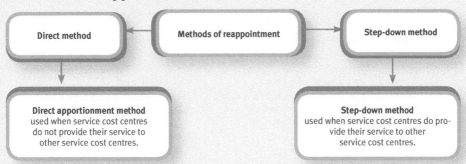

Direct method ← Methods of reappointment → Step-down method

Direct apportionment method used when service cost centres do not provide their service to other service cost centres.

Step-down method used when service cost centres do provide their service to other service cost centres.

Key Point

Aims of reapportionment

The reasons for reapportioning service department overheads is so that all costs are identified with a production cost centre and we can then work out the cost of the units produced by each production cost centre.

Absorption of overheads

Key Point

Having collected all overheads in the production cost centres via overhead allocation, apportionment and reapportionment, the total overhead must be charged to the output of production cost centres. The charging of overhead costs to cost units is called **overhead absorption**.

Absorption rate bases

Various overhead absorption rates exist and the most suitable one should be selected. The use of an absorption rate per unit is for one-product businesses but the following bases may be more appropriate for a multi-product business:

- Absorption rate per direct labour hour.
- Absorption rate per direct machine hour.

Direct labour hour rates are commonly used in labour-intensive production whereas direct machine hour rates are commonly used in machine-intensive production.

Under/over absorption of overheads

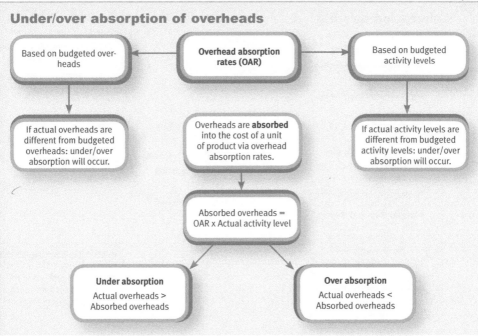

Based on budgeted overheads ← **Overhead absorption rates (OAR)** → Based on budgeted activity levels

If actual overheads are different from budgeted overheads: under/over absorption will occur.

Overheads are **absorbed** into the cost of a unit of product via overhead absorption rates.

If actual activity levels are different from budgeted activity levels: under/over absorption will occur.

Absorbed overheads = OAR x Actual activity level

Under absorption
Actual overheads > Absorbed overheads

Over absorption
Actual overheads < Absorbed overheads

Absorption costing

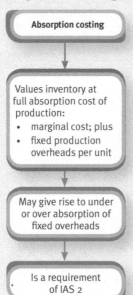

Absorption costing

↓

Values inventory at full absorption cost of production:
- marginal cost; plus
- fixed production overheads per unit

↓

May give rise to under or over absorption of fixed overheads

↓

Is a requirement of IAS 2

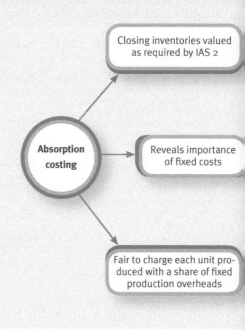

Absorption costing

Closing inventories valued as required by IAS 2

Reveals importance of fixed costs

Fair to charge each unit produced with a share of fixed production overheads

Marginal costing

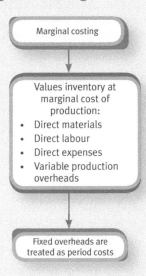

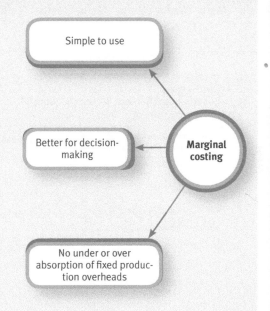

Marginal versus absorption costing

CBA focus

If you are not given opening inventory in a question, assume it equals 0 units.

The difference in inventory valuation between marginal and absorption costing gives rise to a difference in reported profits if there is a movement in inventory levels.

Fixed overhead per unit

$$\frac{\text{Budgeted fixed overheads}}{\text{Budgeted production}}$$

$$\frac{£40,000}{10,000} = £4 \text{ per unit}$$

Example – reported profits

	£ per unit
Sales price	15
Materials	4
Variable production costs	2
Budgeted fixed production overheads	£40,000
Budgeted production	10,000 units
Budgeted sales	8,000 units

Contribution per unit

	£
Sales price	15
Materials	(4)
Variable costs	(2)
Contribution	9

Profit per unit

	£ per unit
Sales price	15
Materials	(4)
Variable costs	(2)
Fixed overhead	(4)
Profit	5

Activity Based Costing

Activity based costing (ABC) is an alternative approach to product costing. It is a form of absorption costing, but, rather than absorbing overheads on a production volume basis it firstly allocates them to cost pools before absorbing them into units using cost drivers.

- A cost pool is an activity that consumes resources and for which overhead costs are identified and allocated. For each cost pool there should be a cost driver.

- A cost driver is a unit of activity that consumes resources. An alternative definition of a cost driver is the factor influencing the level of cost.

Calculating the overhead recovery rate using ABC

There are five basic steps to calculating an activity based cost:

Step 1: Group production overheads into activities, according to how they are driven.

Step 2: Identify cost drivers for each activity, i.e. what causes these activity costs to be incurred.

Step 3: Calculate a cost driver rate for each activity.

Step 4: Absorb the activity costs into the product.

Step 5: Calculate the overhead cost per unit of product

Job costing

Definition

Job costing: the costing system used for a business where production is made up of individual, different, large jobs.

Businesses that use job costing

- Construction companies
- Aeroplane manufacturers
- Vehicle repairers.

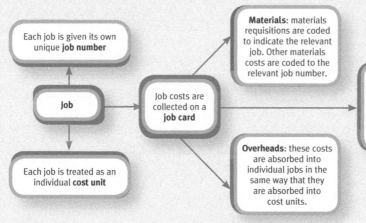

Each job is given its own unique **job number**

Job

Each job is treated as an individual **cost unit**

Job costs are collected on a **job card**

Materials: materials requisitions are coded to indicate the relevant job. Other materials costs are coded to the relevant job number.

Labour: employees working on individual jobs keep job time records and the cost of each employee for each job is recorded on the job card.

Overheads: these costs are absorbed into individual jobs in the same way that they are absorbed into cost units.

Batch costing

Definition

Batch costing: the costing system used for a business where production is made up of different product batches of identical units.

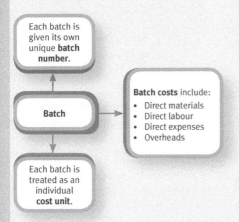

Each batch is given its own unique **batch number.**

Batch

Batch costs include:
- Direct materials
- Direct labour
- Direct expenses
- Overheads

Each batch is treated as an individual **cost unit.**

Service costing

Definition

Service costing is a form of **continuous operation costing**.

The output from a service industry differs from manufacturing for the following four reasons:

- **Intangibility** – the output is in the form of 'performance' rather than tangible or touchable goods or products.
- **Heterogeneity** – the nature and standard of the service will be variable due to the high human input.
- **Simultaneous production and consumption** – the service that you require cannot be inspected in advance of receiving it.
- **Perishability** – the services that you require cannot be stored.

Basics of process costing

Definition

Process costing is the costing method applicable where goods or services result from a sequence of continuous or repetitive operations or processes.

Examples of industries that use process costing:

- Chemical.
- Cement.
- Oil.
- Paint.
- Textile.

Process costing is very similar to batch costing.

$$\text{Cost per unit} = \frac{\text{Net cost of input}}{\text{Expected output}}$$

Normal losses and abnormal loss and gains

Normal loss

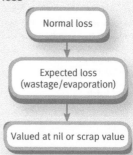

Normal loss

↓

Expected loss (wastage/evaporation)

↓

Valued at nil or scrap value

Normal loss units

1,000 kg or materials were input to a process. Normal loss is expected to be 20% of input.

Normal loss $= 20\% \times 1{,}000 \text{ kg} = 200 \text{ kg}$

Expected output $= \text{Input} - \text{Normal loss}$

$= 1{,}000 \text{ kg} - 200 \text{ kg}$

$= 800 \text{ kg} (80\% \times 1{,}000 \text{ kg})$

Abnormal loss

Abnormal gain

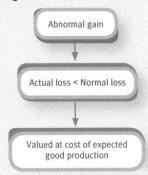

Scrap value

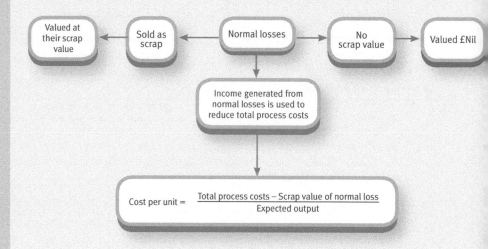

Equivalent units and work in progress

Equivalent units (EUs)

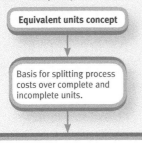

Equivalent units concept

Basis for splitting process costs over complete and incomplete units.

Example – EUs

1,000 units are 50% complete at the end of a period.

EUs = 1,000 x 50% = 500 EUs

Therefore, 1,000 units 50% complete are the same as 500 fully completed units.

Cost per equivalent unit

- Calculated as: $\dfrac{\text{Total cost}}{\text{Number of EUs produced}}$

Summary

- Calculate total EUs.
- Calculate total costs.
- Calculate cost per EU.

Opening Work-In-Progress

AVCO	FIFO
• Include the OWIP carry forward cost in the valuation of the cost per EU	• Split the completed units into 'completed OWIP' and those that were worked from 'start to finish'
	• Include the number of EU required to complete the OWIP in the statement
	• OWIP carry forward costs are included at the valuation of output stage

Relevant costing

Any form of decision-making process involves making a choice between two or more alternatives. Decisions will be taken using relevant costs and revenues.

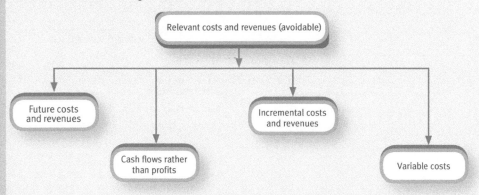

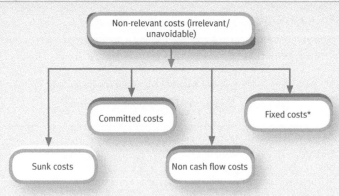

*Note It should be understood that in the long term (by definition) all cost are variable.

Cost-Volume-Profit (CVP) analysis

Definition

Cost-Volume-Profit (CVP) analysis:
analysis of the effects of changes of volume on contribution and profit.

Questions answered by CVP analysis:

- How many units do we need to sell to make a profit?
- How much will profit fall by if the price is reduced by £1?
- What will happen to profits if we rent an extra factory and find we can only operate at half capacity?

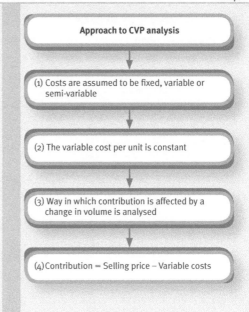

Approach to CVP analysis

⬇

(1) Costs are assumed to be fixed, variable or semi-variable

⬇

(2) The variable cost per unit is constant

⬇

(3) Way in which contribution is affected by a change in volume is analysed

⬇

(4) Contribution = Selling price – Variable costs

Breakeven analysis

Breakeven point

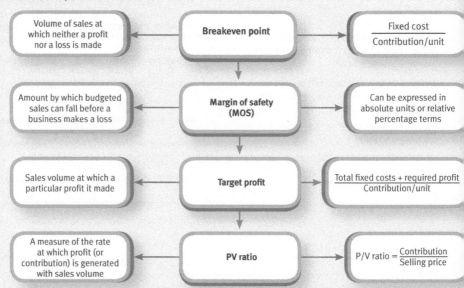

Breakeven point

Volume of sales at which neither a profit nor a loss is made

$$\frac{\text{Fixed cost}}{\text{Contribution/unit}}$$

Margin of safety (MOS)

Amount by which budgeted sales can fall before a business makes a loss

Can be expressed in absolute units or relative percentage terms

Target profit

Sales volume at which a particular profit it made

$$\frac{\text{Total fixed costs} + \text{required profit}}{\text{Contribution/unit}}$$

PV ratio

A measure of the rate at which profit (or contribution) is generated with sales volume

$$\text{P/V ratio} = \frac{\text{Contribution}}{\text{Selling price}}$$

Limiting factors

Limiting factor analysis is a technique used when we have one resource that is in scarce supply and we can make more than one type of product using that resource. Limiting factor analysis determines how to use this resource in such a way that profits are maximised.

Approach to Limiting factor analysis

(1) Determine the limiting factor that is in scarce supply

(2) Calculate the contribution per unit generated by each product

$$\frac{\text{Contribution per unit}}{\text{Number of units of resource needed}}$$

(3) Calculate the contribution per unit of scarce resource for each product

(4) Select the product with the highest contribution per unit of scarce resource and make this first

Net present value (NPV)

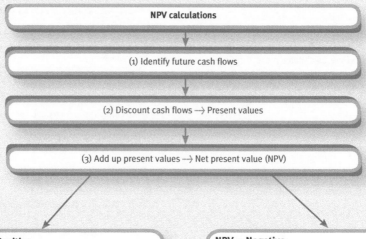

NPV calculations

↓

(1) Identify future cash flows

↓

(2) Discount cash flows ---→ Present values

↓

(3) Add up present values ---→ Net present value (NPV)

NPV = Positive
- Accept project
- PV Cash inflows > PV Cash outflows

NPV = Negative
- Reject project.
- PV Cash outflows > PV Cash inflows

Internal rate of return (IRR)

Definition

IRR: the breakeven cost of capital for one investment opportunity. It is the interest rate or discount factor that means that the investment makes no profit or loss i.e. the NPV of the investment = 0

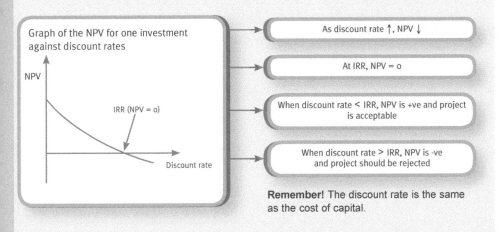

Graph of the NPV for one investment against discount rates

As discount rate ↑, NPV ↓

At IRR, NPV = 0

When discount rate < IRR, NPV is +ve and project is acceptable

When discount rate > IRR, NPV is -ve and project should be rejected

Remember! The discount rate is the same as the cost of capital.

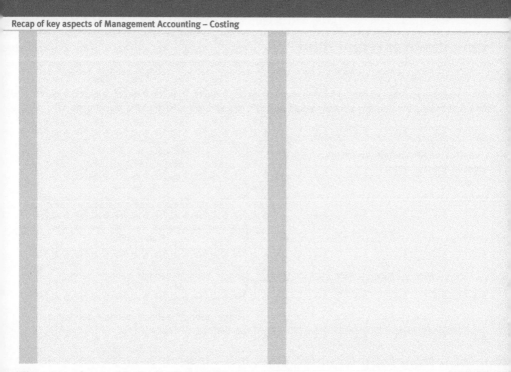

14

Recap of key aspects of Advanced Bookkeeping

- Accounting equation.
- Ledger accounts.
- General rules of double entry bookkeeping.
- IAS16 Property, plant and equipment.
- Capital and revenue expenditure.
- Accounting for depreciation charge.
- Accounting for disposals.
- Part-exchange.
- Purpose of an extended trial balance.
- Layout of an extended trial balance.
- Errors.

- Suspense account.
- Accounting for opening and closing inventory.
- Valuation of closing inventory.
- Irrecoverable and doubtful debts.
- Types of allowance for doubtful debts.
- Recovery of debts.
- Sales ledger control account reconciliation.
- Purchase ledger control account reconciliation.
- Bank control account reconciliation.
- Accruals.
- Miscellaneous income accounts.

Accounting equation

Assets – Liabilities = Capital

Terminology

Asset Something owned by the business	**Liability** Something owed by the business	**Capital** Amount the owner has invested in the business	**Receivable** Someone who owes the business money	**Payable** Someone the business owes money to

Ledger accounts

Typical ledger account:

Title of account

Date	Narrative	£	Date	Narrative	£
	Debit side	x		**Credit** side	x

The dual effect means that every transaction is recorded as a debit in one account and a credit in another account.

Key question – which account is the debit entry to and which account is the credit entry to?

General rules of double entry bookkeeping

Ledger account

Debit	Credit
Money in	Money out
Increase in asset	Increase in liability
Decrease in liability	Decrease in asset
Increase in expense	Increase in income

IAS 16 Property, plant and equipment

- covers accounting treatment of tangible non-current assets and depreciation.

Non-current assets = Long-term assets of the business

Tangible non-current assets = Long-term assets with physical form

Capital and revenue expenditure

Capital expenditure

Revenue expenditure

- expenditure to acquire/enhance economic benefits of non-current assets
- recorded in statement of financial position

- all other expenditure
- charged to statement of profit or loss

Accounting for capital expenditure

Initial purchase:

Debit   Non-current asset account

Credit Bank account/payables account with cost of non-current asset

What is depreciation?

Definition of depreciation

- measure of the cost of the economic benefits of non-current assets that have been consumed during the period
- consumption includes wearing out, using up or other reduction in the useful economic life of the non-current asset whether arising from use, effluxion of time or obsolescence.

Aim of depreciation

- to spread the cost of the non-current asset over its useful economic life.

Accounting concept relating to depreciation

- accruals concept
- charging the cost of the non-current asset to the statement of profit or loss over the period in which it is earning revenue from the non-current asset.

Calculating the depreciation charge

Three methods for AVBK

Straight line   Units of Production   Diminishing (reducing) balance

Accounting for depreciation charge

Depreciation charge – two effects:

Expense in the statement of profit or loss

Reduction in value of asset in statement of financial position

Double entry:

Debit   Depreciation charge account

Credit   Accumulated depreciation account

Accounting for disposals

Two effects of disposal

Asset must be removed from statement of financial position
- remove asset at cost
- remove accumulated depreciation

Account for gain or loss on disposal recognised in the statement of profit or loss
- difference between proceeds and carrying amount

Entries made in disposal account

Part-exchange

Business

Wants to acquire new asset.

Offers old asset in part-exchange.

Pays for remaining cost of new asset.

Part-exchange allowance/value

- effectively proceeds of old asset disposal.
- also part of cost of new asset.

Dealer

Agrees to take old asset in part-exchange.

Values old asset and gives part-exchange allowance.

Purpose of an extended trial balance

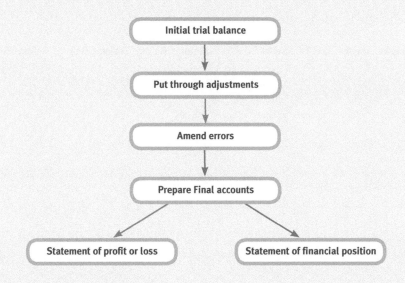

Layout of an extended trial balance

Typical ETB:

Account name	Trial balance		Adjustments		Statement of profit or loss		Statement of financial position	
	DR	CR	DR	CR	DR	CR	DR	CR
	£	£	£	£	£	£	£	£

Errors

In a manual accounting system, errors will be made – some are identified by extracting a trial balance but others will not be.

Single entry

- only one side of an entry made

Casting error

- account incorrectly balanced

> **ERRORS IDENTIFIED BY EXTRACTING A TRIAL BALANCE**

Transposition error

- numbers transposed in recording i.e. 98 shown as 89

Extraction error

- account balance entered on trial balance as wrong figure

Errors of original entry

- error made when transaction first entered into primary records

Compensating errors

- two or more errors which are exactly equal and opposite

ERRORS NOT IDENTIFIED BY EXTRACTING A TRIAL BALANCE

Errors of omission

- a transaction is not entered at all in the primary records

Errors of principle

- entry made in fundamentally wrong type of account i.e. revenue expense entered into capital/ non-current asset account

Errors of commission

- entry made in wrong account although account of the correct type i.e. rent expense entered into electricity expense account

Suspense account

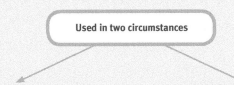

Used in two circumstances

Bookkeeper does not know what to do with one side of an entry and therefore posts it to a suspense account.

Example

£200 received but bookkeeper does not know what it is for so debits cash receipts book and credits suspense account.

When trial balance totals disagree used to balance the trial balance temporarily.

Example

Total of debit balances on trial balance is £35,000 but total of credit balances is £34,000. £1,000 credited to suspense account to make trial balance equal.

Accounting for opening and closing inventory

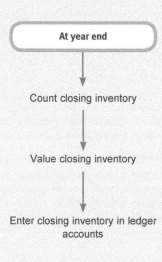

At the beginning of the year

↓

Figure for inventory is always opening inventory

Purchases during year

↓

Always DEBIT purchases

↓

Never make an entry in inventory account

At year end

↓

Count closing inventory

↓

Value closing inventory

↓

Enter closing inventory in ledger accounts

Valuation of closing inventory

Inventory Valuation is the lower of

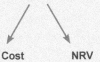

Cost   NRV

- lower of cost and net realisable value
- rule applies to each individual line of inventory.

Cost = expenditure incurred in normal course of business in bringing product to present location and condition.

= • purchase price
  • import duties
  • transport/handling costs
  • direct production costs
  • other overheads attributable to
  • bringing product to present location and condition.

Net realisable value = sales proceeds expected from future sale after deducting any further costs to completion and selling costs.

Irrecoverable and doubtful debts

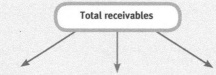

Irrecoverable debts (Bad debts)

- debts highly unlikely to be received
- written off

Doubtful debts

- debts which may not be received
- allowance made and shown in statement of financial position

Good debts

- debts which are highly likely to be received
- shown as current asset in statement of financial position

Types of allowance for doubtful debts

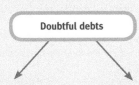

Specific allowance
- particular debt is identified as doubtful e.g. debt from Mr F

General allowance
- business experience indicates that a certain % of debts may not be paid e.g. 5%

Recovery of debts

Debt previously written off

- debt is written off in one year
- in a later year it is unexpectedly received.

Double entry

Debit	Cash/bank account
Credit	Irrecoverable debts expense account

Debt previously provided for

- debt has allowance made against it in one year
- in a later year it is unexpectedly received
- debt is still in SLCA as it has not been written off.

Double entry

Debit	Cash/bank account
Credit	Sales ledger control account

Sales ledger control account reconciliation

SLCA balance = **Total of list of subsidiary (sales) ledger balances**

Purpose of sales ledger control account reconciliation

- to show that the balance in the SLCA does in fact equal the total of the list of balances
- to indicate that there are errors in either the SLCA or the subsidiary (sales) ledger accounts if the two are not equal
- to find the correct figure for total receivables to appear in the trial balance.

Preparing a sales ledger control account reconciliation.

Step 1
- extract list of balances from the subsidiary (sales).

Step 2
- balance the sales ledger control account.

Step 3
- If the two figures are different, the reasons for the difference must be investigated.

Step 4
- correct any errors that affect the sales ledger control account
- find corrected balance on the sales ledger control account.

Step 5
- correct any errors that affect the total of the list of balances from the subsidiary (sales) ledger
- find corrected total of list of subsidiary (sales) ledger balances.

Purchases ledger control account reconciliation

PLCA balance **=** **Total of list of subsidiary (purchases) ledger balances**

Purpose of purchases ledger control account reconciliation

- to show that PLCA does in fact equal the total of the list of balances
- to indicate that there are errors in either the PLCA or the subsidiary (purchases) ledger accounts if the two are not equal
- to find the correct figure for total payables to appear in the trial balance.

Step 1
- extract list of balances from subsidiary (purchases) ledger accounts and total.

Step 2
- balance the purchases ledger control account.

Step 3
- if the two figures are different the reasons for the difference must be investigated.

Step 4
- correct any errors that affect the purchases ledger control account
- find corrected balance on purchases ledger control account.

Step 5
- correct any errors that affect the total of the list of balances from the subsidiary purchases ledger
- find corrected total of list of subsidiary purchases ledger balances.

Bank control account reconciliation

At regular intervals the cashier must check that the cash book is correct by comparing the cash book with the bank statement.

Why might they not agree?

Cheques we've paid in have not yet been cleared = "uncleared lodgements"
(Bank statement not fully up to date – our records fine).

Cheques we have written have not yet been taken to bank by the recipients or have not yet cleared = "unpresented cheques"
(Bank statement not fully up to date – our records fine).

Bank Charges / Interest we haven't accounted for (need to update our records for these).

Example

The following differences have been identified when comparing the cash book with the bank statements.

(i) Bank interest received £80, had not been entered in the cashbook
(ii) A BACS receipt of £12,400 and £920 from two customers has not been entered in the cashbook
(iii) A receipt for £1,300 has been recorded in the cashbook as £1,500
(iv) Cheques drawn for £7,880 entered in the cashbook are not showing on the bank statement.

Using the table below show those items that would be required to update the cashbook.

Adjustment	Amount £	Debit	Credit
(i)	80	✓	
(ii)	13,320	✓	
(iii)	200		✓

Accruals

Accruals concept

Income/expenses dealt with in statement of profit or loss in period in which earned/incurred not period in which cash received/paid

Accrual = expense incurred not yet paid for

Prepayment = expense paid for but not yet incurred

Miscellaneous income accounts

- e.g. rent received
- income credited to SPL is amount earned in period not cash received

Cash received>income earned=income prepaid

Cash received<income earned=income accrued

15

Recap of key aspects of Final Accounts Preparation

- Capital accounts.
- Current accounts.
- Appropriation account.
- Statement of financial position presentation.
- Admission of a partner.
- Retirement of a partner.
- Incomplete records – Net Assets approach.

- Use of control accounts.
- Mark-ups and margins.
- Gross sales margin percentage.
- The regulatory framework.
- The underlying assumptions.
- The fundamental qualitative characteristics.

Capital accounts

- one for each partner (generally columnar)
- only generally used when partners pay capital into the business.

Debit   Cash/bank

Credit   Capital account

Current accounts

- one for each partner (generally columnar)
- used for transactions between partnership and partners

Current accounts

DEBIT	CREDIT
Drawings	Salaries to partners
	Interest on capital
	Profit share

- normally a small credit balance being amount partnership owes to partners.

Appropriation account

- used to share out net profit to partners
- according to profit share agreement.

Statement of financial position presentation

- capital accounts and current accounts balanced
- balances shown in bottom part of statement of financial position.

Example

Capital accounts

	A £	B £		A £	B £
			Balance b/d	30,000	20,000

Current accounts

	A £	B £		A £	B £
Drawings	25,000	20,000	Balance b/d	1,000	1,500
			Salary		8,000
			Interest on capital	1,500	1,000
Balance b/d	2,500	3,000	Profit share	25,000	12,500
	27,500	23,000		27,500	23,000
			Balance b/d	2,500	3,000

Statement of financial position – extract

	£	£
Total net assets (bal fig)		55,500
Capital		
Capital accounts – A		30,000
Capital accounts – B		20,000
		50,000
Capital accounts – A	2,500	
Capital accounts – B	3,000	
		5,500
		55,500

Admission of a Partner

NEW PARTNER ADMITTED

Pays capital into partnership

Buying a share of net assets of partnership

Also buying a share of goodwill, which is unrecorded in the SFP

Retirement of a partner

PARTNER RETIRES

Calculate all that is due to him
- capital a/c balance
- current a/c balance
- share of goodwill

Pay off partner/ leave money on loan to partnership/pay in cash/or both

Incomplete records – Net Assets approach

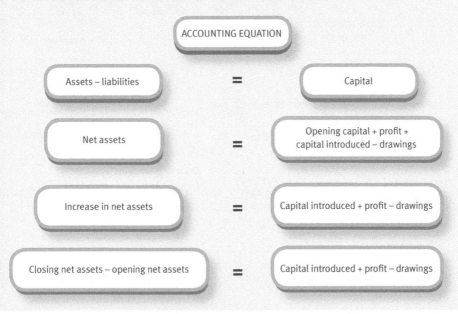

ACCOUNTING EQUATION

| Assets – liabilities | = | Capital |

| Net assets | = | Opening capital + profit + capital introduced – drawings |

| Increase in net assets | = | Capital introduced + profit – drawings |

| Closing net assets – opening net assets | = | Capital introduced + profit – drawings |

Use of control accounts

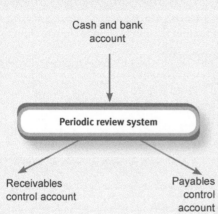

Cash and bank account

Periodic review system

Receivables control account

Payables control account

Cash/bank account

- used to find missing figures such as cash takings/cash drawings.

Sales ledger control account

	£		£
Opening balance	X	Bank receipts	X
Sales	X	Discount allowed	X
	X	Sales returns	X
	X	Bad debts written off	X
	X	Contra with PLCA	X
		Closing balance	X
	X		X

Purchase ledger control account

	£		£
Bank payments	X	Opening balance	X
Purchase returns	X	Purchases	X
Discounts received	X		
Contra with SLCA	X		
Closing balance	X		
	X		X

If three of the four figures are known, the fourth can be found as the balancing figure.

Mark-ups and margins

- cost structures provide a link between
  selling price and cost.

Mark-up	Margins
% added to cost to find selling price	gross profit as a % of selling price

Gross sales margin percentage

The gross sales profit margin percentage
shows the percentage of profit retained from
the selling price after deducting the cost of
producing that good or service. This can be
calculated as:

$$\frac{\text{Gross Profit}}{\text{Sales}} \times 100$$

The regulatory framework

All UK companies may use **International Financial Reporting Standards (IFRSs)** when preparing their financial statements. It is mandatory for listed UK companies to use IFRS.

Accounting standards give guidance in specific areas of accounting.

IFRSs are issued by the **International Accounting Standards Board (IASB)**.

The **IFRS Interpretations committee (IFRS IC)** assist the IASB in establishing and improving standards of financial accounting and reporting.

The **IFRS Advisory Council (IFRS AC)** provides a forum for organisations and individuals to input into the standard setting process.

Outlined below are three accounting standards which AAT may test as part of the Final Accounts Preparation unit:

IAS 1 Presentation of the Financial Statements

This accounting standard sets out the overall requirements for financial statements for organisations adopting IFRSs, including how they should be structured, the minimum requirements for their content and overriding concepts such as going concern, the accruals basis of accounting and the format and classification of financial statements. The standard requires a complete set of financial statements to comprise a statement of financial position, a statement of profit or loss and other comprehensive income, a statement of changes in equity and a statement of cash flows.

IAS 2 Inventories

This accounting standard contains the requirements on how to account for most types of inventory. The standard requires inventories to be measured at the lower of cost and net realisable value (NRV).

IAS 16 Property, Plant and Equipment

This accounting standard outlines the accounting treatment for most types of property, plant and equipment. Property, plant and equipment is measured at its cost and depreciated so that its depreciable amount is allocated over its useful economic life.

The underlying assumptions

Going concern basis assumes that the business will continue in operational existence for the foreseeable future without the need or intention to cease trading.

Accruals basis ensures that transactions are reflected in the financial statements for the period in which they occur. This means that the amount of income should be recognised as it is earned and expenses when they are incurred.

The fundamental qualitative characteristics

The framework identifies two fundamental qualitative characteristics of useful financial information. Preparers of the financial information should attempt to maximise these characteristics to benefit the users of the accounts.

Relevance ensures that the information is capable of influencing the decision-making of the users of the financial information.

Faithful representation ensures that the information is complete, neutral and free from error.

There are also four supporting qualitative characteristics:

Comparability – it should be possible to compare an entity over time and with similar information about other entities.

Verifiability – if information can be verified (e.g. through an audit) this provides assurance to the users that it is both credible and reliable.

Timeliness – information should be provided to users within a timescale suitable for their decision making purposes.

Understandability – information should be understandable to those that might want to review and use it. This can be facilitated through appropriate classification, characterisation and presentation of information.

Index